HOW TO THINK

# CREATIVE THINKING PUZZLES

## BRAIN-TRAINING PUZZLES TO IMPROVE INNOVATIVE THOUGHT

CHARLES PHILLIPS

WELBECK

# CONTENTS

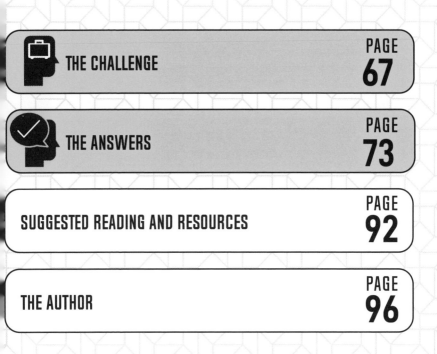

## HOW TO THINK CREATIVELY

Do you want to express yourself? Do you want to be more creative? This book will show you how, revealing simple strategies to free up the creativity you have within you and explaining how to harness its power at work, at college or in everyday life.

Many people underestimate their own powers of creativity. Perhaps because they have never really tried to be creative or have suffered setbacks when they have tried, they believe creative thinking and its rewards are set aside for other people. Yet we can all train ourselves in any kind of mental activity – and creative thinking is no exception.

We each possess immensely powerful and malleable brains, and all of us have an enormous capacity to change and to learn. Each human brain contains one hundred billion brain cells (neurons) and every neuron can make connections with thousands or tens of thousands of others. Each second a brain makes a million new connections – so once we commit to a project and persevere with it, we can make astonishing progress!

If, up to now, you've tended to think creativity was for others, it's time to realize you can train yourself to think in a more creative way. If you already feel quite confident of your creativity, you can develop your skills much further. Start now, using the carefully designed puzzles in this book, and building on the tips and strategies spread throughout.

Of course, creative ideas and the drive to self-expression come and go. Some days you'll certainly be more creative than others. And there are a number of ways you can prime yourself to be creative. So read on …

## BE POSITIVE

The first key step is to accept that like any other person you are naturally creative, and that you can learn techniques and methods to enhance your creativity. Think positive – one of the main bars to creativity is a fear of making mistakes. Believe in yourself. Calm the critical inner voice that can paralyze inventive thinking. And if you're managing or leading people at work or in another context, and you want to boost their creativity, be encouraging and give positive feedback on their ideas or work.

## EMBRACE CHANGE

A good way to encourage creativity is to stimulate yourself through change. Even in the smallest things, change can boost your thinking. Move your desk at work or in your study; change your morning routine, if you can, by walking and taking the bus instead of driving to your destination; try changing your hairstyle or your look or taking a short break somewhere.

## AND TALK!

Scientists tell us that our brains are often more active when we are working with others. Take advantage of the benefits of cooperative thinking. Talk as much as you can – to other people when shopping, to friends or family over dinner, even to yourself as you work.

The psychologist and author Edward de Bono devised a useful set of questioning strategies to be used by different parts of your thinking mind .These are intended to develop ideas by focusing on, for example, your forward-looking and optimistic side – you could say, "Let's list the good aspects of this idea." Or to address your emotional side you could say, "What do you find exciting or frightening about this?" Or to question your logical side you could ask, "Am I sure that A follows from B?"

## RELAX AND SEE THE FUNNY SIDE

You're more likely to be creative when you're relaxed. Simple breathing exercises and meditation can help prepare you to be creative. And laughter is a great primer for creativity. Make jokes, seek out books and movies that make you laugh, and – if you can – spend time with people you find funny. Brain scientists report that laughter, and the relaxation that follows it, shunts your brain from short, high-frequency brainwaves to the longer, slower waves that generally accompany creative thought.

# INTRODUCTION

## THE PUZZLES IN THIS BOOK

There are three levels of puzzles, each with a "time to beat" deadline. These deadlines apply a little pressure – we often think better when we have goals such as time constraints. But don't worry – if you find you take longer than the "ideal" time, relax. And some puzzles have a similar version later in the book to give you more practise.

Look out for puzzles marked Time Plus. You'll need a bit longer to complete these – not because they are more difficult as problems but because there's more work to do before you can solve them. Where we feel you might need some help, a tip has been provided, and there are Notes and Scribbles pages later on for note-making and scribbling! Also toward the end of the book, the Challenge is designed to give your newly acquired skills a good, solid workout. This has a suggested time limit of 10–15 minutes to give you a chance to think around and away from the problem, perhaps making a few notes in the margin.

Don't rush. Take as long as you want if you are faced with a particularly challenging problem – the important thing is to try to think in the way outlined, to practise those creative-thinking skills. You'll find as your new skills develop that you quickly see the effect at work or in a class, and in other areas of your life – by showing yourself to be resourceful, being quick to adapt and proving yourself equal to challenges. So, start thinking creatively, and turn the page!

| PUZZLE GRADING | TIME TO BEAT |
|---|---|
| EASY = WARM-UP | 1–2 MINUTES |
| MEDIUM = WORKOUT | 3–4 MINUTES |
| DIFFICULT = WORK HARDER | 5–6 MINUTES |
| TIME-PLUS PUZZLES | 6+ MINUTES |
| THE CHALLENGE | 10–15 MINUTES |

# 50
## PUZZLES
## FOR
## CREATIVE
## THINKING

**REMEMBER.** Relax! Be positive. Don't get stuck in a rut. Talk to yourself and others. Believe in your mind and set it free to think **CREATIVELY**

# EASY PUZZLES

## FOR CREATIVE THINKING

The puzzles in this first section of the book give your creative-thinking skills a warm-up. The ability to think visually is a key part of being creative, and these puzzles are designed to stretch your powers of observation and visualization. Look as closely as you can at the artworks and puzzles – and also look beyond what you see. Try to view the problems with fresh eyes, from unconventional angles. Don't be afraid to consider the impossible – and think around the challenges. Take a step sideways and surprise yourself.

11

## PUZZLE 1
# BAGUETTE BONANZA

Christophe, a French baker, is pedalling through his beautiful village, humming the "Marseillaise" with a basket of fresh baguettes. He is stopped by one of his best customers, Brigitte, who buys half his loaves, plus half a loaf. Then the local priest, Father Albert, stops him and does the same – he buys half Christophe's stock, and a further half baguette. Finally, a young boy, Vincent, repeats the order – half Christophe's bread plus half a loaf more. Christophe is delighted – he has sold all his bread, and yet he has not had to break a baguette. Can you work out how this is possible, and how many loaves he must have started with?

# HOW TO
# THINK
## TIP

Get counting – but think creatively about the numbers in question.

12

## PUZZLE 2
# COLONEL OLIVER

Which of the four portraits of Colonel Oliver marked A–D in the box (below, right) should fill the empty space in the matrix?

Think about how the colonel's appearance changes.

## PUZZLE 3
# PATH OF 3

How's your mental maths? Can you find your way from any square on the top row of the grid to any square on the bottom, passing only through numbers that will divide exactly by three? Diagonal moves are not allowed.

| 44 | 87 | 14 | 76 | 52 | 27 | 70 | 85 | 43 |
|----|----|----|----|----|----|----|----|----|
| 64 | 48 | 44 | 12 | 9  | 42 | 75 | 35 | 45 |
| 14 | 51 | 46 | 79 | 49 | 16 | 54 | 56 | 75 |
| 8  | 15 | 72 | 63 | 27 | 74 | 42 | 38 | 78 |
| 16 | 21 | 55 | 50 | 57 | 67 | 43 | 44 | 93 |
| 18 | 24 | 22 | 51 | 99 | 81 | 75 | 91 | 18 |
| 21 | 79 | 77 | 31 | 16 | 17 | 24 | 94 | 27 |
| 90 | 89 | 96 | 84 | 93 | 69 | 42 | 73 | 48 |
| 26 | 91 | 54 | 53 | 65 | 88 | 58 | 19 | 12 |

# HOW TO
# THINK
### TIP

**If the sum of the digits of a number is divisible by three, then the number is divisible by three.**

## PUZZLE 4
# LETTER DICE

When the diagram (below, left) is folded to form a cube, just one of the five letter-dice on its right (A-E) can be produced. But which one?

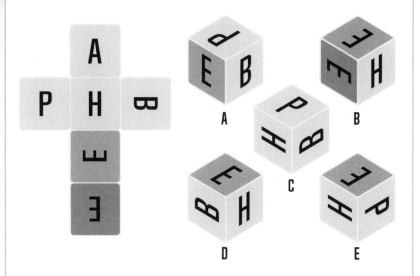

A

B

C

D

E

## HOW TO THINK TIP

Think about which letters you'll find on adjoining faces on the finished die. When you've done this puzzle, can you come up with a good game to play with a set of letter dice?

## PUZZLE 5
# AN OUTSTANDING VASE

One of these vases is different from the others. Can you decide which one stands out? The ability to focus your attention and see differences quickly is a key aspect of all kinds of thinking.

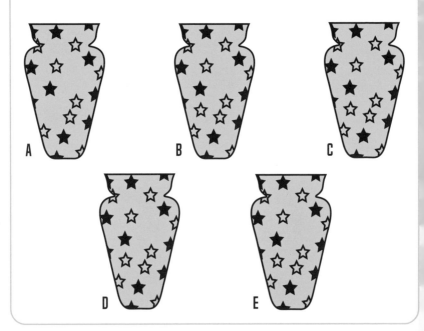

A    B    C

D    E

 **HOW TO THINK TIP**

Look closely – then look again. You could try counting the stars.

16

## PUZZLE 6
# MISS SHAW'S SHAPES

Miss Shaw's eight-year-old schoolchildren have grown very skilled at cutting out shapes with scissors. She keeps the cut-outs in her desk drawer. For parents' evening, she will put the shapes out on display, but she does not want any repeating shapes. When she opens the drawer, this is what she sees. Can you help find the one shape that appears twice in her drawer?

**HOW TO THINK TIP**

You'll need a keen eye to do this puzzle, especially within the time limit, because some shapes overlap others.

## PUZZLE 7
# ASHLEY SMELLS PIZZA

Ashley and his parents visit a large country house with a maze in the garden. When his parents enter the maze, Ashley runs off into the trees after their dog, Bruno. Now he finds the maze. Can you help him make his way from the opening at top left to the one at the bottom right? He's quite keen to get through because the visitors' cafe is right by the maze exit and he can smell delicious pizza, so you need to help him find the quickest route.

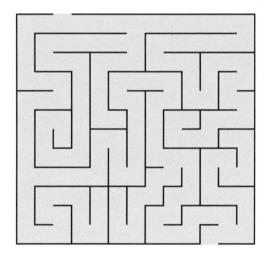

**HOW TO THINK TIP**

For this, the first maze in the book, you may find it easier to trace the path using a pencil rather than depending on your eyes alone.

## PUZZLE 8
# TROUBLESOME TIMEPIECE

Dexter's watch gains four minutes every hour. He last checked the watch and put it right at 11 am today. Now it is 4.15 pm – but what time does Dexter's watch show?

 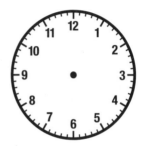

## PUZZLE 9
# TAKE YOUR TIME, MAGGIE

Maggie hates ironing, but she finds that it's just about bearable if she irons for 10 minutes, then takes a five-minute break, then irons for 10 minutes and takes another five-minute break – and so on. In her latest ironing session, yesterday, she ironed for a total of two hours (not including her breaks). She started at 11.15 am: What time did she finish ironing?

 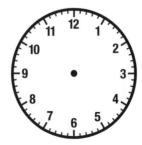

## PUZZLE 10
# SYMBOL SUDOKU

Can you fill up the grid so that every column and row contains one and one only of each of the six symbols? This puzzle works just like a conventional numerical sudoku, except that the numbers are replaced with the six symbols shown.

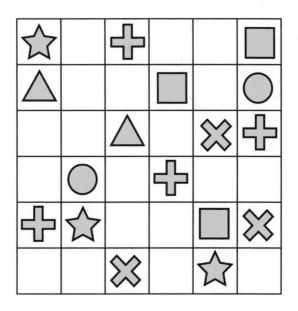

**HOW TO THINK TIP**

**Begin by scanning the rows and columns to see if you can spot any obvious missing symbols.**

## PUZZLE 11
# DAMIAN'S DOMINO WALL

As a test for his brother, Declan, Damian builds a wall from 10 dominoes, then masks seven of them out. Can you help Declan place the missing dominoes provided below in their correct places? You must bear in mind the following rules laid down by Damian: first, each vertical line of four numbers (as well as the two end vertical lines of two numbers) adds up to eight; secondly, the second from top horizontal row of dominoes adds up to 17; and thirdly, the third horizontal row of dominoes has dots totalling five.

**HOW TO THINK TIP**

Once you're sure of the position of a domino, it may help to score through it, so that you don't place the same domino twice.

21

## PUZZLE 12
# SNAKES AND LADDERS

On a train journey, Serena and Augustus decide to play a game of Snakes and Ladders. But they have to devise a special version since, although they have a board, they don't have any pieces or a die. So they ask their friend, Shusuke, to imagine they are throwing a die and write down the scores. Shusuke plans the whole game out for them and tells them how good it will be for their thinking skills to play it in their minds rather than by using physical pieces. Unfortunately, the game ends in a big argument that disturbs the other train passengers because Augustus and Serena can't agree who has won.

Can you help them decide the winner? These are the rules and the numbers determined by Shusuke.

Augustus throws the first 6 so starts first, placing his counter on the 6. After that, every time it is Serena's turn to play, her die follows the sequence 6, 4, 2, 5, 3, 1; so her first move is to square number 6, then square number 10 and so on. After Augustus's first turn, when he throws the 6, his die follows the sequence 2, 4, 6, 1, 3, 5, so his second move is to square number 8, his third is to number 12 and so on. Serena and Augustus follow the normal rules of the game: Whenever one of them lands on a square with the foot of a ladder, the counter is moved (in their imagination) to the top of the ladder; and whenever one of them lands on a square with the head of a snake, the counter is moved to the tail of the snake. The number thrown to end the game doesn't matter, since the first to reach 100 on the board wins.

| 100 | 99 | 98 | 97 | 96 | 95 | 94 | 93 | 92 | 91 |
|-----|----|----|----|----|----|----|----|----|----|
| 81 | 82 | 83 | 84 | 85 | 86 | 87 | 88 | 89 | 90 |
| 80 | 79 | 78 | 77 | 76 | 75 | 74 | 73 | 72 | 71 |
| 61 | 62 | 63 | 64 | 65 | 66 | 67 | 68 | 69 | 70 |
| 60 | 59 | 58 | 57 | 56 | 55 | 54 | 53 | 52 | 51 |
| 41 | 42 | 43 | 44 | 45 | 46 | 47 | 48 | 49 | 50 |
| 40 | 39 | 38 | 37 | 36 | 35 | 34 | 33 | 32 | 31 |
| 21 | 22 | 23 | 24 | 25 | 26 | 27 | 28 | 29 | 30 |
| 20 | 19 | 18 | 17 | 16 | 15 | 14 | 13 | 12 | 11 |
| 1 | 2 | 3 | 4 | 5 | 6 | 7 | 8 | 9 | 10 |

**HOW TO THINK TIP**

This is a Time-Plus puzzle, because there's a good deal of working out to do before you can solve the puzzle. It's best if – like Serena and Augustus – you can plot the moves of the game in your head, but even if you physically work them out on the printed board, the puzzle still provides good exercise for your visualization skills and for your memory.

## PUZZLE 13
# WHEELY DIFFERENT

Alejandro loves his motorbike. Here are five pictures of him riding it that provide a spot the difference puzzle with a twist. The challenge is not, as is usual with these puzzles, to find the one example that is different from the others – in this version, each picture of Alejandro has one thing distinguishing him from the others. Can you spot the one difference in each case?

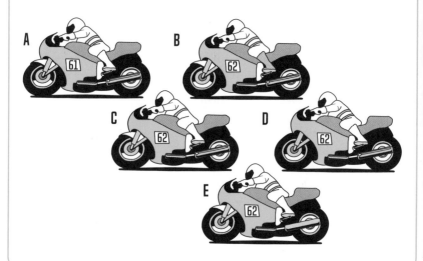

**HOW TO THINK TIP**

Start by looking at just two of the bikes only, to give your eyes and your brain time to absorb the different elements.

## PUZZLE 14
# FULL STEAM AHEAD

Ana is drawing pictures of a steam train for a children's book called *Full Steam Ahead*, which she is writing with her sister, Maria. When Maria asks for two identical pictures, Ana copies one exactly. But then unfortunately she drops the pile of pictures. Can you help her sort out the two in the set that are identical?

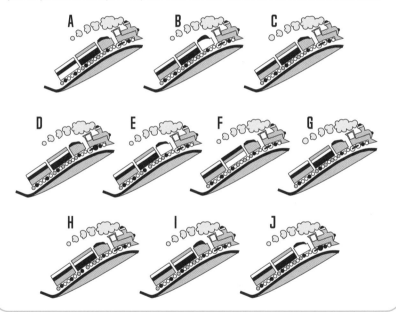

 **HOW TO THINK TIP**

A good starting point is to eliminate the ones that are obviously different, then you can concentrate on those with more subtle differences without feeling overwhelmed.

## PUZZLE 15
# BATTLESHIPS

This is the first of a group of puzzles in the book that are based on the well-known game of battleships, familiar since at least the era of the First World War. In our version, the numbers on the side and bottom of the grid indicate occupied squares or groups of consecutive occupied squares in each row or column. Can you fill up the grid so that it contains three cruisers, three launches and three buoys – and the numbers are all correct?

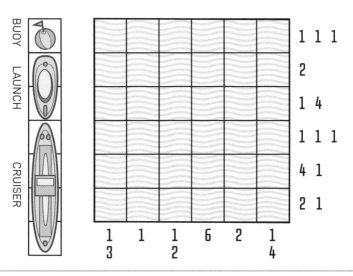

**HOW TO**
**THINK**
**TIP**

Think about how many ways there are to occupy four consecutive squares with the objects provided.

26

## PUZZLE 16
# MISS SHAW'S SHAPES 2

Miss Shaw is still busy preparing for her school parents' evening (see Puzzle 6). In a second drawer, she finds the circles, squares, triangles and stars below, which her children cut out during a creative maths class. This time, her colleague Mr Schumm asks her to divide the shapes with two thin sticks, one going from top to bottom and one from side to side, to create four areas, each containing four different orange shapes (star, circle, triangle and square) and four different white shapes (star, circle, triangle and square). How did she do it?

 **HOW TO THINK TIP**

Focus on one shape first, such as the square, and try to create four areas that each contain one example.

27

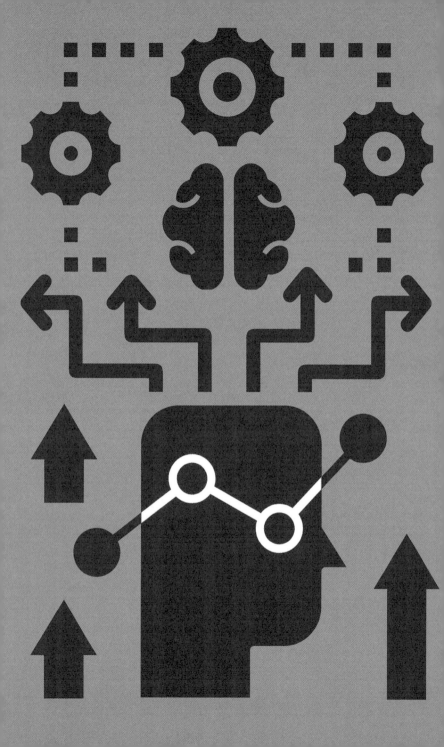

# MEDIUM PUZZLES

## FOR CREATIVE THINKING

 **WORKOUT**

This second section contains medium-difficulty puzzles designed to provide a more demanding workout for your creative thinking. By now you're probably feeling more at home with your powers of creative thought, and more confident of your ability to think your way around a challenge. Don't forget the benefits of talking – talk to yourself, aloud if you can! Ask yourself "what if" and "why not" questions about the puzzles. Verbalizing in this way focuses the mind, and these private conversations have a way of throwing up new ideas. Suddenly, as is the way with creative thinking, the solution may jump out at you.

## PUZZLE 17
# PROFESSOR GREENACRE'S BISCUITS

Professor Greenacre has two great loves: geometry and baking. He also takes pleasure in giving his friends tests of their visual intelligence when they visit. Today he has baked some biscuits using his several different-shaped cutters and arranged them carefully in sequential patterns on his four pentagonal baking trays. Then he withdraws one tray from the sequence and hides it, and draws the four plans A, B, C and D shown below. "Which of the four plans," he asks his friend Dr Gupta, "shows the missing pattern?"

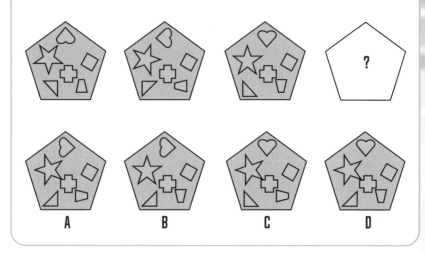

A          B          C          D

**HOW TO THINK TIP**

As Dr Gupta strokes his beard, he looks at the alignment of the shapes.

PUZZLE 18
# CAMP CONIFER

Camp Conifer is a well-spaced campsite. Every camper has plenty of shade, and so remains happy despite the searing heat. Look at the grid map of the site, showing the location of its trees. Next to every tree, draw a tent. Each tent should be either immediately above, below or beside its tree, and no two tents can be on adjacent squares (even diagonally). The numbers at the end of each row and column tell you how many tents the row or column must contain.

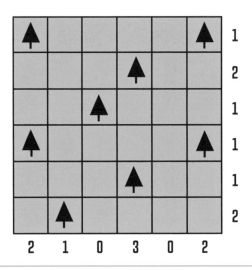

## HOW TO THINK TIP

As in many creative-thinking tasks, it pays to consider the implications before jumping to a conclusion.

## PUZZLE 19
# MR SCHUMM'S NUMBER MAZE

Miss Shaw's (see Puzzle 16) fellow teacher Mr Schumm has a class full of children who love maths. To entertain them he has drawn a number maze in the playground. He tells them, "Make your way from the top to the bottom of the number maze, without passing through the same square more than once, and creating a working sum as you go!" He offers a punnet of strawberries as prize. One of his brightest pupils, Astrid, wins the strawberries. Can you see which path Astrid follows?

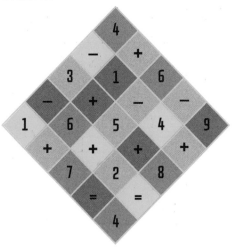

## HOW TO
# THINK
### TIP

Your path may not always head directly to the solution – be prepared to meander a bit.

## PUZZLE 20
# MIRROR IMAGE

When completed, this picture is perfectly symmetrical around a vertical line drawn straight down the middle. Can you generate two matching halves that complete the picture?

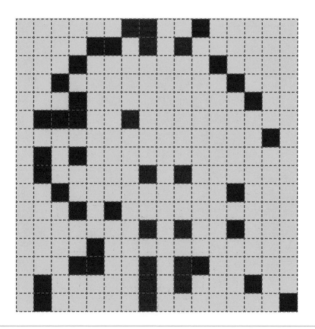

 **HOW TO THINK TIP**

The puzzle is a simple test of logic combined with visualization – once you have identified the central line, you need only add squares matching those already provided.

## PUZZLE 21
# ASHLEY WINS AN ICE CREAM

After Ashley and his parents finish their pizza (see Puzzle 7), they discover a second, more complicated maze on the other side of the country house they are visiting. His parents decide to take a rest in the sunshine with their dog, Bruno, but Ashley is keen to try the maze, so his father Andy makes him an offer. If he can find his way through the maze in 3–4 minutes, he will be rewarded with an ice cream from the food stall by the lake. In this maze, the entrance is at the top right and the exit is almost directly beneath it at the bottom right.

 **HOW TO THINK TIP**

No pens allowed! Try following Ashley's route with your eyes only to hone that creative brain.

## PUZZLE 22
# MISS SHAW'S SHAPES 3

Miss Shaw has found another container full of shapes to sort (see Puzzles 6 and 16). This time she wants to find a pair of shapes to add to a special display. Can you help her find the only shape to appear twice in the set below? The parents are arriving at the school and she must find them within 3–4 minutes, so she can make it to the door to welcome the firstcomers!

**Remember to look out for shapes that overlap.**

## PUZZLE 23
# ANDREA'S VASES

Andrea the potter is delivering an order of four identical vases to a new downtown restaurant named Giovanni's and one slightly different vase to an art gallery called Magenta. At the last minute, with her vehicle blocking one lane on a busy road outside Magenta and cars honking loudly at her, she finds that she has got the vases muddled up. Can you help her find the slightly different vase intended for Magenta?

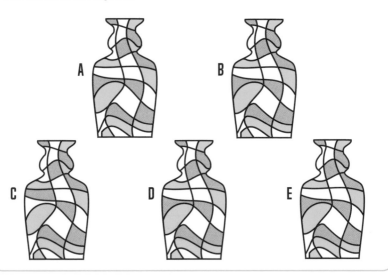

 **HOW TO THINK TIP**

Check each vase's outline, examining the different panels one by one.

36

## PUZZLE 24
# NATE'S TILES

Nate is putting up a section of expensive handmade tiles for a Mexican bar. But he is called away by a family crisis, leaving his assistant Hugo to finish the job. Hugo has to choose the correct set from the groups of tiles shown below right (A–D) to complete the matrix pattern Nate has begun. Can you help him?

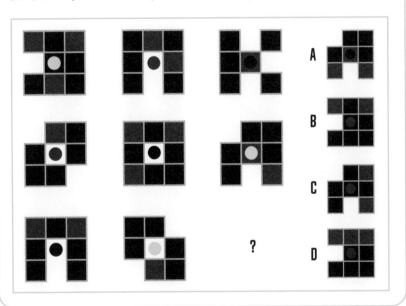

 **HOW TO THINK TIP**

Think about whether you should look at rows or columns, or both together.

## PUZZLE 25
# NUMBER BOX

When the diagram below is folded to form a cube, only one of the following options can be produced. Which one is correct?

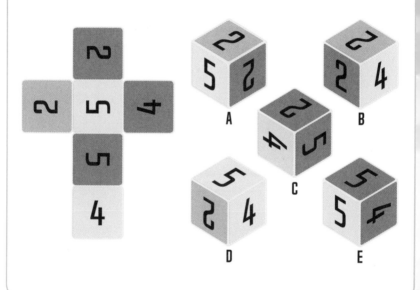

**HOW TO**
# THINK
## TIP

Try visualizing which numbers will fall on adjoining sides of the cube.

38

## PUZZLE 26
# LIFE

In Chip's educational video game, Life, a mad scientist has developed a new medium called "watair" that combines the qualities of water and air. In the box of "watair" below, fish live happily alongside ants and butterflies. The challenge is to use just three straight lines to divide this square into five areas, each of which contains just one butterfly, one ant and one fish.

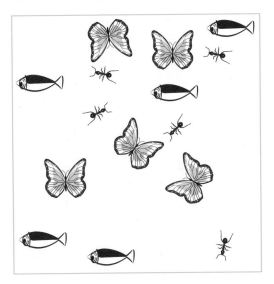

 **HOW TO THINK TIP**

**Should the lines cross? What do you think?**

## PUZZLE 27
# HIDDEN PICTURE

Can you find your way home to the solution of this puzzle? To do so, colour in some squares on the grid to create an image. The numbers outside the grid refer to the number of consecutive coloured squares from left to right or top to bottom, and each block of coloured squares is separated from the others by at least one white square. For instance, 3, 2 could refer to a column with none, one or more white squares, then three coloured squares, at least one white square, two more coloured squares, followed by any number of white squares.

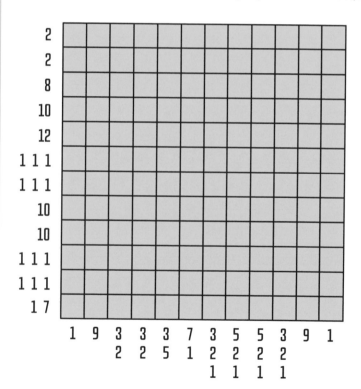

## PUZZLE 28
# DORA'S DOLLS

Isadora has a treasured set of nine rag dolls, each one of which is different from the others. For her birthday, her friend Tom gives her a new doll that is identical to one in the set. She keeps them separate, but one day her mother is tidying the house and mixes the dolls up in a toy box. Can you help Dora find the two dolls that are identical in the toy box?

Don't be put off by the number of dolls – concentrate on one feature only to start with, such as hair colour. As you eliminate some, the puzzle will seem more manageable.

## PUZZLE 29
# SYMBOL SUDOKU 2

Here's another sudoku puzzle with a twist. As in Puzzle 10, you are asked to complete the grid like a conventional numerical sudoku but using symbols rather than numbers. This time, to make the puzzle harder, there are nine rather than the six symbols we used in Puzzle 8. The task here is to fill up the grid so that every column, row and small square contains one each of the nine symbols.

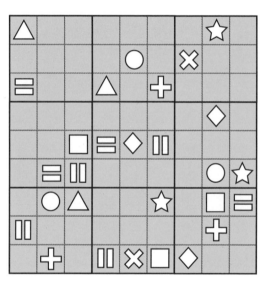

**HOW TO THINK TIP**

As with all sudokus, if you first spot any obvious gaps, the rest will start to fall into place.

## PUZZLE 30
# DECLAN'S DOMINO CHALLENGE

This time Declan devised a test for Damian (see Puzzle 11). He drew the design below and asked Damian: "Can you fit four different dominoes into the square below, so that the horizontal and vertical sides of the square each total seven?" He went on: "I've placed two dominoes in their correct positions, but I haven't revealed how many spots (there are no blank faces) should be on the second faces of these dominoes. You'll need to work this out, as well as the locations of the other dominoes."

**HOW TO THINK TIP**

Because there are just four dominoes, this puzzle seems simpler than it is. Don't be put off if you can't find the solution immediately.

## PUZZLE 31
# THE CLOCKS IN LECTURE HALL H

Professor Alexis loves Lecture Hall H, because it has no fewer than five clocks on the wall behind the lectern. Today, for his maths lecture, he sets the first four clocks to the times shown below. He asks the students: "To complete this sequence, what time should be on the fifth clock?" Only one student, Uma, gets the answer right. What did she say?

## HOW TO
# THINK
### TIP

Time seems to be travelling backward in Professor Alexis's lectures.

## PUZZLE 32
# JOSH'S TRICK BRICKS

Josh is an artist. For his son Kendall, he makes a neat set of letter bricks in which some bricks have tiny individual differences. He arranges five sets of three bricks as shown below, so that in each set one brick differs in one way from the others. Can you help Kendall spot the one difference in every case?

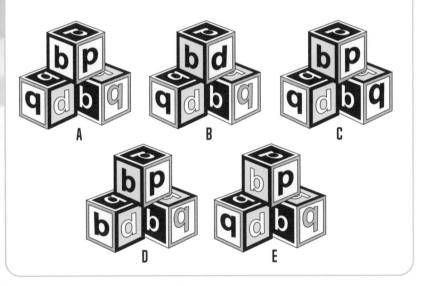

A        B        C

D        E

**HOW TO**
**THINK**
**TIP**

How good are your powers of observation? Look at the outlines and backgrounds as well as the letters on the bricks.

## PUZZLE 33
# BATTLESHIPS 2

Here's another chance to try your hand at our version of the game of battleships (see Puzzle 15). As before, the numbers on the side and bottom of the grid indicate occupied squares or groups of consecutive occupied squares in each row or column. Can you fill up the grid so that it contains three cruisers, three launches and three buoys and the numbers all correspond with the occupied squares?

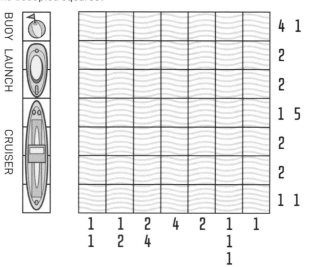

BUOY  LAUNCH    CRUISER

4 1

2

2

1 5

2

2

1 1

1 1 2 4 2 1 1
1 2 4     1
            1

## HOW TO
# THINK
### TIP

**Think horizontally as well as vertically.**

46

## PUZZLE 34
# EDWIN AND MRS SIMPSON

The highly eccentric Edwin, Earl of Glossop, passed away. Before he died, in his will, he left 21 sausages to his pregnant golden retriever, "Mrs Simpson." His will dictated that if Mrs Simpson's puppy were male, then the retriever should inherit seven sausages and the young puppy should receive the remaining 14. If the puppy were female, however, Mrs Simpson should receive 14 sausages and the female puppy should have 7. As things transpired, Mrs Simpson had two puppies, one of each sex. How on earth could the Earl's scrupulous solicitors divide up the sausages according to his last wishes?

 **HOW TO THINK TIP**

As with earlier puzzles of this kind, try turning the book around in your hands to see the shape from different angles – or try visualizing it from a lateral (sideways) perspective or from behind.

# DIFFICULT PUZZLES

## FOR CREATIVE THINKING

 **WORK HARDER**

You'll have to work harder to solve the puzzles in this third part of the book, which contains the most demanding of our exercises in creative thinking. But, paradoxically, the best approach is to banish the idea of "hard work" before you start. Remember the benefits of being relaxed and in the right frame of mind. Take some deep breaths and close your eyes for a few minutes first. Concentrate – but don't try too hard. Aim to connect with your intuition. Consider your first response carefully, or any answer that seems to come to you unbidden. If it's not the right answer itself, it may contain the seeds of a useful response.

## PUZZLE 35
# ASHLEY WINS A SCHOOL PRIZE

With happy memories of his adventures on his weekend visit to the country house (see Puzzles 7 and 21), Ashley devises the maze shown below for his maths homework. These are the instructions he provides: "Find your way from the top to the bottom of the maze, without recrossing your path, and collecting numbers that added together total exactly 20."

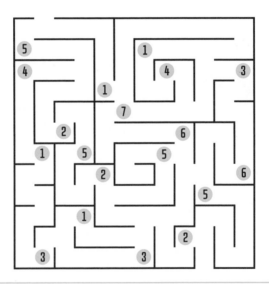

**HOW TO THINK TIP**

Use visual logic alongside simple maths. Because it combines activities in this way, Ashley's maze is a good example of cross training for the brain, which scientists report to be highly stimulating and likely to promote powerful thinking.

## PUZZLE 36
# STAR BAR

Piotr is a designer. He has a hit with a series of star symbols used on T-shirts and hats. For a new client he makes a linked set for the wall of an upscale eating and drinking venue, the Star Bar. He leaves the designs with the bar manager, Patrick, along with a few spares. But Patrick gets one of the designs muddled up with the spares. Which of the four boxed designs (A–D) completes the sequence of designs in the matrix and should be used to fill the empty space?

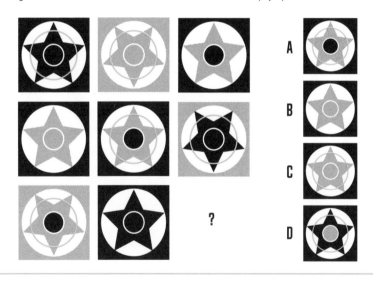

**HOW TO THINK TIP**

Piotr tries to suggest a subliminal funky and "alternative" atmosphere by inverting some of the symbols.

## PUZZLE 37
# MIRROR IMAGE 2

Like Puzzle 20, this picture, when finished, is perfectly symmetrical around a vertical line drawn straight down the middle. Identify the line, then plot new squares to match exactly the existing ones on the other side of the line. As you work, an image will appear before your eyes.

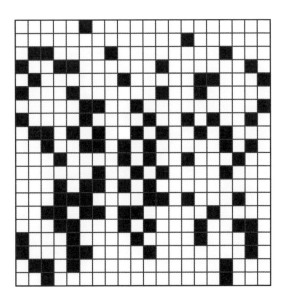

**HOW TO THINK TIP**

First find the line of symmetry, and the rest will quickly follow.

## PUZZLE 38
# CHURCH STARS

Piotr has made some more of his star-based designs (see Puzzle 36), this time for a fundraiser at his church. He made a large printout of the five designs, then he asked the members of the public to identify which one of the five designs is different from all the others.

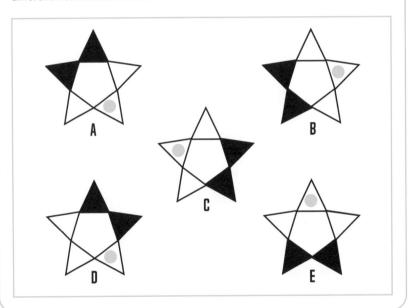

**HOW TO THINK TIP**

Approach this puzzle from all angles.

## PUZZLE 39
# MEHNDI MAZE

Inspired by mehndi art (fine temporary tattoos drawn in henna, usually on the palms and feet), Jasmine devised the intricate maze drawn below for a maths-influenced art project. "It works like an ordinary maze," she told her art teacher Ms Jones. "You have to find your way through from the entrance to the exit as quickly as possible." The entrance is near the top right.

## HOW TO
# THINK
### TIP

**Found the exit? It's near the bottom right. This is a Time-Plus Puzzle, since it demands a good amount of trial and error, and perseverance – as well as a pen or pencil.**

## PUZZLE 40
# LETTER DICE 2

Here's another test of your ability to think visually in three dimensions.
Like Puzzles 4 and 25, this asks you to imagine folding the diagram below on the left to make a cube. When you do so, which of the five cubes shown on its right (A–E) will be produced?

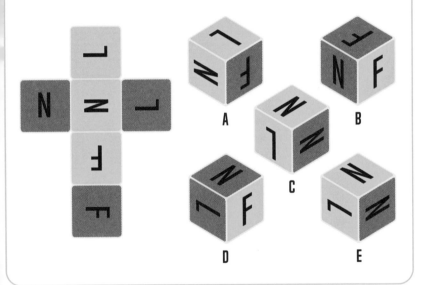

 **HOW TO THINK TIP**

Try to solve the puzzle using your mind's eye only. But if you're really stumped, you could try making your own cube!

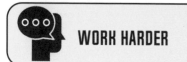
## PUZZLE 41
# MISS SHAW'S SHAPES 4

This is our final visit to Miss Shaw's classroom (see Puzzles 6, 16 and 23). She's found one more drawer that needs sorting. Once again, she wants to find the one shape that appears twice in the box.

**HOW TO THINK TIP**

As before, watch out for rotated images. Study the picture closely. Sometimes it helps to look away, rest your eyes, take a few deep breaths – then look intently again.

## PUZZLE 42
# SNOW CROWD

Donna, Everett, Ella, Rocco and Heath stage a snowman-building contest one day in the school's playground. Antonio, the janitor, lends the children hats and brooms. "Look!" says Ella, "We've made a snow crowd!" Each snowman differs in one way from the others. Can you spot the one difference in every case?

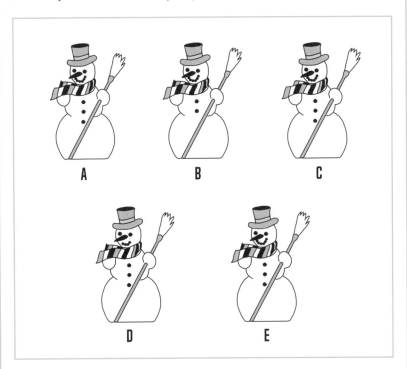

## PUZZLE 43
# GREEN ACRE'S CHOCOLATE CHALLENGE

Professor Greenacre, who loves to combine geometry and cooking (see Puzzle 17), produces these designs made from white and brown chocolates for the faculty Christmas party. He hides the fourth design and draws the four alternatives, then asks his colleagues which of the four, A–D, would complete the sequence below? He offers the chocolates to the winner. Dr Mukherjee of the English department is the first with the correct answer and she enters into the spirit of the season by sharing her prize of chocolates with all her colleagues. What was her answer?

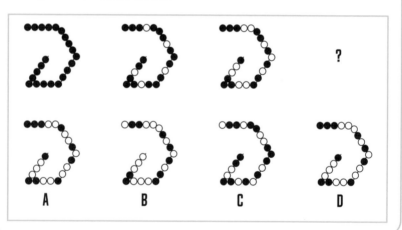

# HOW TO
# THINK
## TIP

It may help you to know that Professor Greenacre loves patterns as well as shapes.

## PUZZLE 44
# THE FLY-BY-NIGHTS

One dark night Sir Peter's house is burgled. The thieves must be specialists, for the only thing they steal is a rare and extremely valuable Picasso. Two days later, Sir Peter receives a ransom note telling him to buy a diamond worth a million dollars, and to take it to a telephone box in a near by park at midnight – or else he will never see the painting again. Sir Peter is prepared to do as he is told, but he first makes sure that the park is surrounded by hidden police, ready to capture the thieves when they try to leave the area with the diamond. Sir Peter takes the diamond to the park, finds the telephone box and opens the door. Immediately he realizes that the police aren't going to catch the thieves.

How does Sir Peter know this? What is in the telephone box?

**HOW TO THINK TIP**

The thieves applied their powers of creative thinking to the problem of how to get the diamond safely out of the park.

## PUZZLE 45
# THE CLOCKS IN THE COLLEGE BOATHOUSE

Professor Alexis (see Puzzle 31) is very popular with his maths students. Two of them, Jem and Ty, devised this time challenge for him using the clocks in the college boathouse, where he goes to train each morning. The fifth clock in the sequence is broken, so they have removed its hands. They ask him, "Following the sequence from left to right, what time should be showing on the clock bottom right?"

Can time go backwards as well as forward?

## PUZZLE 46
# HIDDEN PICTURE 2

Here's a chance to build on the plotting and visualization skills you developed in Puzzle 27. This is a more demanding test still and, as before, is a Time-Plus puzzle because it requires patient work. The rules are as follows: the numbers outside the grid refer to the number of consecutive coloured squares from left to right or top to bottom; each block is separated from the others by at least one white square. For instance, 3, 2 could refer to a row with none, one or more white squares, then three coloured squares, at least one white square, two more coloured squares, followed by any number of white squares.

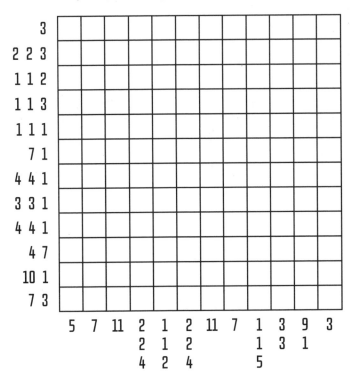

## PUZZLE 47
# LIBRARY TILES

Marco is an interior designer and maker of tiles. He made these letter tiles to decorate the library in his client Justina's house. Marco's assistant, Arvo, is a linguist and adds a sequencing to the letters. As a game, he arranges the four variants, A–D, below, and asks Marco which one he should use to complete the sequence.

| F | L | P |
|---|---|---|
| E | Y | K |
| M | D | H |

| H | N | R |
|---|---|---|
| D | X | J |
| L | C | G |

| J | P | T |
|---|---|---|
| C | W | I |
| K | B | F |

|   |
|---|
| ? |
|   |

| L | R | W |
|---|---|---|
| B | V | H |
| J | A | E |

**A**

| L | R | V |
|---|---|---|
| B | V | H |
| J | A | E |

**B**

| L | R | V |
|---|---|---|
| A | V | H |
| J | A | E |

**C**

| L | R | V |
|---|---|---|
| B | U | H |
| J | A | E |

**D**

# HOW TO
# THINK
# TIP

Are the sequences different in different rows?

## PUZZLE 48
# SYMBOL SUDOKU 3

This gives you a third chance to have a go at our intriguing Symbol Sudokus – sudoku puzzles with a twist. As in Puzzles 10 and 29, you are asked to complete the grid like a conventional numerical sudoku but using symbols rather than numbers. Fill up the grid so that every column, row and small square of nine blocks contains one each of the nine symbols.

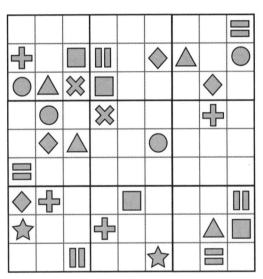

It won't take a minute to copy the puzzle onto a piece of paper – then you can attempt it on the paper and leave the original free to be tried again. It's worth returning to the puzzles in the book, and a good exercise of your creative powers to devise your own versions of them for your friends.

## PUZZLE 49
# BATTLESHIPS 3

Like Puzzles 15 and 33, this game is based on the traditional paper and pencil game of battleships and provides valuable practise in devising and projecting visual combinations. As before, the numbers on the side and bottom of the grid indicate occupied squares or groups of consecutive occupied squares in each row or column. Can you fill up the grid so that it contains four cruisers, four launches, and four buoys and the numbers outside the grid are all correct?

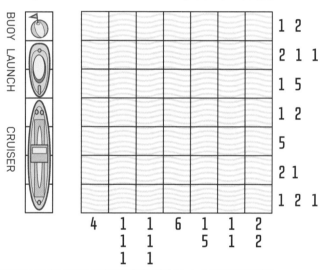

## PUZZLE 50
# PROFESSOR GREENACRE'S CUPCAKES

Professor Greenacre is up to his old tricks again (see Puzzles 17 and 43), bringing geometry into the kitchen. He has baked a set of 24 cupcakes, this time using his star, circle and square moulds. Twelve cakes are dark (topped with chocolate) and twelve are light (with vanilla icing). He has arranged them very carefully on his favourite tray (which is in the shape of an ellipse). He asks his guest, Henri, who is visiting from France, whether he can – using just two straight lines – divide the ellipse into three areas, each containing one light-coloured square cake, two dark star cakes, two dark circular cakes and three light-coloured circular cakes. Can you?

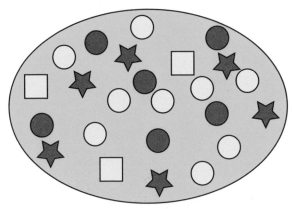

**HOW TO**
**THINK**
**TIP**

Try using a pencil and ruler as dividers.

# THE CHALLENGE

This final section of the book gives you an opportunity to put the creative-thinking skills you have developed into practise by overcoming several challenges to your creativity in an almost-real setting. At this level of creative thinking, it can help to think of the task and of life situations as a game. Try to consider the rules and if could you change them. In this exercise, and more generally, it is also an aid to practical creativity to develop the habit of interrogating your thinking. Take a step back and consider: how are you thinking, are you being creative and could you be more playful and intuitive?

# A WORKING BIRTHDAY

The scenario that follows gives you a series of light-hearted tests of your creative-thinking skills and a chance to try out strategies and tips for creativity that you have picked up in the course of the book. In this scenario, you suffer an alarming intervention that leaves you with nothing but your wits to survive on – the challenge is to work out creative solutions to the problems that present themselves in the course of what is a highly demanding morning. By the end you may be ready to work out why and by whom this intervention was made.

Over the following pages, then, be ready to look beyond surface appearances. Read the text through three or four times, noting down clues and ideas in the side columns provided. Accept ambiguities; consider implausible solutions. It may be a useful strategy to "think the opposite" – to state your position in reverse, or try deliberately to think what you don't believe. Ask plenty of questions. Be flexible. Be willing to change strategy and head off in a new direction if one doesn't work. All these approaches are really worth practising – they will boost your performance in meeting challenges and finding solutions at work, school and in other real-life situations. So, take a deep breath, prepare yourself to be creative and read on ...

This could be the worst birthday of your life.

You are forced to cancel a lunch date with your three sisters, Maureen, Oona and Shona, because you have to make a last-minute business trip to promote your consultancy service, Creative Business Solutions, to a new client – SHOOM! Developments. You are walking to the station when a limousine marked SHOOM! pulls up. The female driver jumps out and says she has been sent to drive you to the presentation.

You are so surprised that you surrender your briefcase to her despite the fact that it has all your personal belongings in it. As she puts the case in the car, you think, "Doesn't she look familiar?" Then she helps you climb into the back of the limo, closes and locks the door after you, and clambers in herself.

She pulls away into the traffic. You try to ask her questions, but she ignores you. Following a brief drive you come into the part of the city where SHOOM! is situated, but the driver takes an unexpected turn and soon you are in an unfamiliar

## NOTES &
## CLUES

district. "Are we lost?" you ask. The driver turns some music on the stereo. It is the classic "Moon River."

You go through mean streets, where young men in baggy shorts and shirts are skateboarding. A couple of the men stare at you; one is dancing to music from a beatbox. Then the driver swings into a deserted multistory parking structure, heading downwards. She drives very fast across the lowest level of the parking structure and stops suddenly beside an elevator, just as the song ends.

She turns the engine off, says "See you up there!", then jumps out of the driver's door, taking your case with her and running away into the gloom.

You try to get out to follow her but find your door is locked. You look around in a panic. The parking structure is deserted. You try to be calm, close your eyes for a few moments and at last study your surroundings.

On the passenger's seat in the front you see an envelope

## NOTES & CLUES

addressed to you. Inside is a sheet of paper headed SHOOM! Developments. It says: "We look forward to meeting, as arranged, at 11 am. Please bring forward creative ideas for redeveloping a large multistory parking facility in a rundown part of the inner city." Stapled to it is what looks like a cloakroom ticket marked "Moon River".

You look at your wristwatch. It is 10.30 am – you have 30 minutes to get to the meeting. Outside, the elevator beside the car has what looks like a number-punch keypad set in the wall – perhaps for entering a code. Above it is a small LCD screen with these words scrolling by on it endlessly "How did you get here? Why are you here?" in green letters.

How can you get out of the car? How will you find the office? What development plan can you come up with for the parking facility if you make the meeting? What do you do, or rather – how do you think?

## NOTES & CLUES

# THE ANSWERS

## CREATIVE THINKING PUZZLES

Try to use this answer section as a source of inspiration. Everyone feels stumped sometimes – when we're fresh out of ideas and need help. If you're really stuck, by all means look up the answer. Then, after reading the solution, rehearse the steps in the creative-thinking process that led to the answer given, so that you adopt the strategy for use with future puzzles and in real life. As with all puzzles, it's possible that you may sometimes find an alternative solution. If so, well done – that's creativity in action!

## PUZZLE 1
## BAGUETTE BONANZA

Christophe started with seven loaves. He sold four to Brigitte, then two to Father Albert and one to Vincent.

## PUZZLE 2
## COLONEL OLIVER

The answer is A. Each row and column in the matrix contains one portrait of the colonel with a white monocle, one with a black monocle and one with no monocle. Each row and column also contains two portraits with hair (the colonel wearing his wig) and one bald head (the colonel in his full glory). Each row and column also contains two portraits of the colonel with a beard and one without. The missing portrait should therefore show the colonel with his favourite black monocle, with his wig on and with a beard.

## PUZZLE 3
## PATH OF 3

See the route shown below. It's worth practising mental maths because the ability to juggle numbers is often required when you're trying to compute various choices in a creative-thinking challenge.

| 44 | 87 | 14 | 76 | 52 | 27 | 70 | 85 | 43 |
| 64 | 48 | 44 | 12 | 9 | 42 | 75 | 35 | 45 |
| 14 | 51 | 46 | 79 | 49 | 16 | 54 | 56 | 75 |
| 8 | 15 | 72 | 63 | 27 | 74 | 42 | 38 | 78 |
| 16 | 21 | 55 | 50 | 57 | 67 | 43 | 44 | 93 |
| 18 | 24 | 22 | 51 | 99 | 81 | 75 | 91 | 18 |
| 21 | 79 | 77 | 31 | 16 | 17 | 24 | 94 | 27 |
| 90 | 89 | 96 | 84 | 93 | 69 | 42 | 73 | 48 |
| 26 | 91 | 54 | 53 | 65 | 88 | 58 | 19 | 12 |

## PUZZLE 4
### LETTER DICE

The answer is D. The letter B will have H and E on neighbouring faces. This puzzle tests your ability to think visually and to plot information in three dimensions. Like mental maths, it's a skill you often need in tests of creative thinking.

## PUZZLE 5
### AN OUTSTANDING VASE

A stands out. The others have an extra star on the left side as shown. Spot the difference puzzles such as this one hone your attention to detail and powers of observation, which you need in creative thinking.

## PUZZLE 6
### MISS SHAW'S SHAPES

The three-pronged shape reproduced below is the only one to appear twice in Miss Shaw's drawer. If you found it within the time limit, you did well. You must have good concentration and visual awareness. These qualities will serve you well in creative-thinking challenges – both in puzzle books and in real life, when you may, for example, have to master and mentally sort visual data quickly for a project at work or a class.

## PUZZLE 7
## ASHLEY SMELLS PIZZA

The quickest route through the maze to the cafe is the one marked on the plan below. When Ashley gets to the cafe, he finds a choice of three pizzas: Pepperoni Plus, Vegetarian Delight and Mexican Maze. He chooses the third and generously shares it with Bruno and his parents.

## PUZZLE 8
## TROUBLESOME TIMEPIECE

The time on the watch is 4.36 pm. The time difference between 11 am and 4.15 pm is five-and-a-quarter hours: Dexter's watch gains four minutes an hour, so in five-and-a-quarter hours it gains 21 minutes, making it 4.36 pm.

## PUZZLE 9
## TAKE YOUR TIME, MAGGIE

In two hours of ironing, Maggie would have twelve 10-minute ironing sessions, with eleven five-minute breaks in between them, making a total of 2 hours 55 minutes. Added to 11.15, this gives a finishing time of 2.10 pm.

## PUZZLE 10
## SYMBOL SUDOKU

The completed symbol sudoku grid is shown below. Creative thinking often requires you to be flexible in approach and to seek out unusual combinations; this lateral twist on a sudoku provides very good practise in these skills.

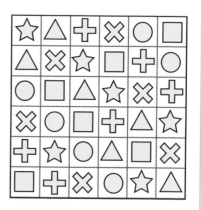

## PUZZLE 11
## DAMIAN'S DOMINO WALL

Damian's domino wall looks like the one reproduced below. Like Puzzle 3, this is an example of a game designed to get you making relatively simple calculations at speed – which has been shown by Japanese brain-training expert Dr Ryuta Kawashima to stimulate your brain, thus boosting the quality of your thinking.

## PUZZLE 12
## SNAKES AND LADDERS

Serena wins the game. She has 22 throws, and her moves are: 6, 10, 12, 17, 20, 21/39, 45, 49, 51, 56, 59, 60, 66, 70, 72, 77, 80/62, 63, 69/89, 93, 95, 100. Augustus's moves are: 6, 8, 12, 18, 19, 22, 27, 29, 33, 39, 40, 43, 48, 50, 54/48, 54/48, 49, 52, 57, 59, 63, 69/89, 90, at which point Serena wins.

## PUZZLE 13
## WHEELY DIFFERENT

In A, Alejandro's bike is number 61, but in the others it is 62. In B, Alejandro's boot is grey rather than white. In C, Alejandro's jacket has one stripe rather than two. In D, the front mudguard is missing. In E, the motorbike's exhaust is missing its shine.

## PUZZLE 14
## FULL STEAM AHEAD

The two identical pictures drawn by Ana are C and G. Keep an eye on the time limit when doing these puzzles, since the ability to identify differences or similarities at speed is a valuable asset for your thinking.

## PUZZLE 15
### BATTLESHIPS

The completed grid is displayed below. You'll see that in the column furthest left there is one single occupied square, then three consecutively occupied squares, matching the numbers at the bottom of the column.

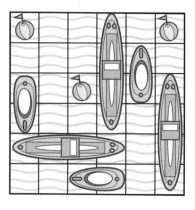

## PUZZLE 16
### MISS SHAW'S SHAPES 2

Miss Shaw divides the shapes in the drawer as shown right. She is a math whiz and does it quickly, but for some of us it can be difficult to see the space between the shapes easily, and the puzzle is a good test within this rather tight time limit; developing and practicing the ability to see patterns and to group objects in this way is good for your visual intelligence.

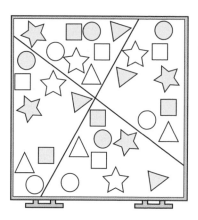

## PUZZLE 17
## PROFESSOR GREENACRE'S BISCUITS

The answer is A. Dr Gupta is delighted to see the pattern. "The white shapes each make a quarter-turn anticlockwise every time," he says. "You don't fool me, Greenacre." The professor smiles quietly and offers Dr Gupta a biscuit. "It's truly a pleasure to see you, Doctor," he smiles.

## PUZZLE 18
## CAMP CONIFER

The completed grid map is shown below. This puzzle is another chance to develop your ability to plot information while visualizing interconnections. Did you learn quite quickly that it's not always good to be hasty?

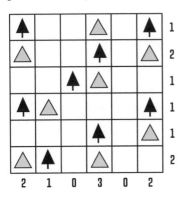

## PUZZLE 19
## MR. SCHUMM'S NUMBER MAZE

The path Astrid follows is shown below. The sum she makes is: $4 + 6 - 5 + 3 - 6 + 2 = 4$. The puzzle combines simple numerical maths with a test of visual logic. Stimulating more than one mental process in the brain builds connections between your neurons and boosts thinking performance.

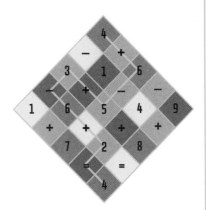

## PUZZLE 20
## MIRROR IMAGE

The completed picture is a facial portrait as shown below. Visual puzzles stimulate many parts of the brain, and while visual stimuli are initially processed in the occipital lobe at the brain's rear, other brain areas further forward come into play to judge shape as well as how things fit together and so on.

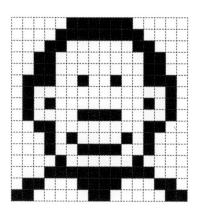

## PUZZLE 21
## ASHLEY WINS AN ICE CREAM

The route Ashley follows is shown below. This is quite a demanding test of your powers of creative visualization. You did well if you managed to complete the maze within the target time of 3–4 minutes. Although Ashley needed 5 minutes, Andy was impressed with his son's efforts and bought him an ice cream anyway.

## PUZZLE 22
## ANDREA'S VASES

The odd one out is C. The area just below the neck of the vase on the left is of a different colour (as circled). In creative thinking, you need to pay attention to detail: be sure of your data before you try leaps of intuition or lateral thinking.

## PUZZLE 23
## MISS SHAW'S SHAPES 3

The four-pronged shape shown right is the only one that appears twice in the container. This is a good test for your powers of observation. Miss Shaw found the matching pair just as the first parents appeared.

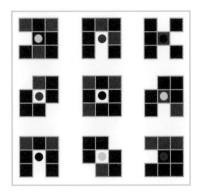

## PUZZLE 24
## NATE'S TILES

The correct answer is D. Each row and column in the matrix pattern contains a design with one grey square, one with two grey squares and one with three grey squares. Each row and column contains a design with one square missing, a design with two squares missing and a design with three squares missing. Each row and column contains a central grey dot, a central orange dot and a central black dot. The missing piece of the matrix must contain three grey squares, one square missing and a central grey dot. Hugo gets it right, and later Nate buys him a beer.

## PUZZLE 25
## NUMBER BOX

The correct answer is A. This is a more demanding version of Letter Dice (Puzzle 4). I find this puzzle harder to solve because it's more tricky to plot the correct position of the numerals than it is to do the same with letters – for example, it's quite easy to become confused about which way up a number 2 is. The puzzle is a good test of creative visualization.

## PUZZLE 26
## LIFE

The lines need to be drawn as shown right to create five "watair" areas of different shapes, each containing one butterfly, one ant, and one fish. Can you think of any other new mediums like the water-air blend of "watair?" Could any of your ideas be useful?

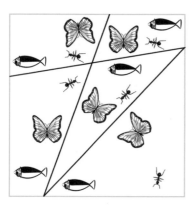

## PUZZLE 27
## HIDDEN PICTURE

Did you make it home? The completed grid is shown below. As specified beside the grid, the top two horizontal rows each contain just two black squares (forming the chimney); the two (vertical) columns at extreme right and left each contain just one black square (forming the guttering).

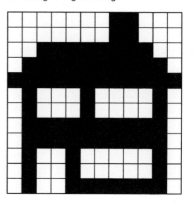

## PUZZLE 28
## DORA'S DOLLS

Doll A and doll I. When you exercise creative thinking, a key skill is to challenge your assumptions. Make sure you see what is there rather than what you assume is there. Time-limited tests give good practise in noticing tiny details.

## PUZZLE 29
### SYMBOL SUDOKU 2

The completed grid is shown below. Many tests of creative thinking involve plotting information, then recognizing, creating or recreating patterns; this puzzle gives you a challenging workout in these types of thinking.

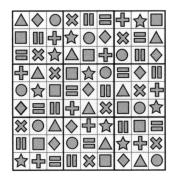

## PUZZLE 30
### DECLAN'S DOMINO CHALLENGE

The solution to Declan's challenge is shown below. The dots on the dominoes add up to seven along both horizontal and vertical edges of the square.

## PUZZLE 31
### THE CLOCKS IN LECTURE HALL H

The correct time is 5.35. Uma compares the time on clocks 2, 3 and 4 with that on clock 1 and works out that, respectively, the clocks show times of minus one hour 10 minutes, minus one hour 20 minutes and minus one hour 30 minutes, so the final clock should show a time of minus one hour and 40 minutes. Clock 4 shows 7.15, and 7.15 minus one hour 40 minutes is 5.35.

## PUZZLE 32
### JOSH'S TRICK BRICKS

In set A, the "b" on the top brick is on a white background. In set B, one of the letters on the top brick has changed from a "p" to a "d." In set C, a "q" on the bottom-right brick has changed to black. In set D, one of the letters on the bottom-left brick has changed from a "q" to a "b." In set E, the "b" on the top brick has changed to a white letter.

# ANSWERS

## PUZZLE 33
## BATTLESHIPS 2

The completed grid is shown below. In the top (horizontal) row, for example, the battleship occupies four consecutive squares and the buoy occupies a single square, matching the numbers 4, 1 beside the grid. The battleships game provides great practise in visualizing groups of shapes and their combination within a constrained space, stimulating areas of the brain's right hemisphere that are essential for critical thinking.

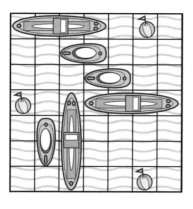

## PUZZLE 34
## EDWIN AND MRS SIMPSON

The Earl's solicitors – reasoning that the Earl wished Mrs Simpson to get twice as many sausages as a female puppy, and half as many as a male puppy – gave Mrs Simpson six sausages, her male puppy 12 and her female puppy three.

## PUZZLE 35
## ASHLEY WINS A SCHOOL PRIZE

This is the route through the maze that Ashley plotted. The numbers add up as follows: 1 + 1 + 4 + 3 + 6 + 5 = 20. Ashley's maths teacher, Mr Carvajal, is very impressed and decides to award him a school prize in maths.

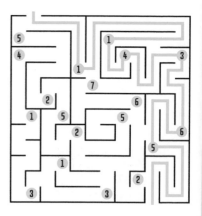

## PUZZLE 36
## STAR BAR

The answer is C. Each row and column contains a design with one grey square and two black ones. Each row and column also contains one black star and two grey ones. Each row and column contains one inverted star and two the right way up. Each row and column contains one central grey circle and two black ones, and each row and column contains two designs with a mid-sized orange circle and one without it. The missing design should therefore have a black square, a grey star (right way up), a central grey circle, and a mid-sized orange circle.

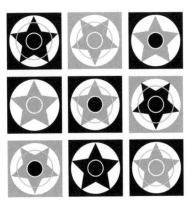

## PUZZLE 37
## MIRROR IMAGE 2

The completed and perfectly symmetrical picture is of a moth or butterfly, as shown right. Like Puzzle 37, this demands concentration and meticulous attention to detail.

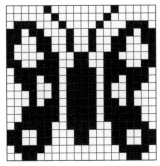

## PUZZLE 38
## CHURCH STARS

The answer is D, as below. Figures B, C and E are all the same as figure A, only rotated. Because the designs look good when rotated, Piotr is considering a design like this for the central label on a record. He may approach some record companies with the idea, now that vinyl is back in fashion.

## PUZZLE 39
## MEHNDI MAZE

The route through Jasmine's maze is as shown below. The perseverance you need to complete this puzzle is essential to creative thinking. In creative tasks, you often have to try one strategy, then another, then perhaps a third or more – without becoming dispirited.

## PUZZLE 40
## LETTER DICE 2

The correct answer is E. When the diagram is folded, the two letter Ns would be in the directions shown right; in answer C, the two Ns are wrongly aligned. Can you devise other puzzles that test similar skills?

## PUZZLE 41
## MISS SHAW'S SHAPES 4

The small four-sided piece, below, is the one repeating piece. Miss Shaw takes the pair of pieces out to show them to a parent interested in discussing pattern recognition. Identifying visual patterns quickly is certainly a skill you can develop with practise.

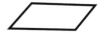

## PUZZLE 42
## SNOW CROWD

In snowman A, made by Donna, the top of the broom is slightly shorter. In snowman B, made by Everett, the lowest button is missing. In snowman C, made by Ella, part of one end of the scarf is missing. In snowman D, made by Rocco, the snowman's mouth is smaller. In snowman E, made by Heath, the scarf is slightly different – with two stripes of a different colour.

## PUZZLE 43
### GREENACRE'S CHOCOLATE CHALLENGE

The correct answer is D.
Dr Mukherjee sees that, in the procession from left to right, counting only the brown buttons, every fourth brown button becomes white.

## PUZZLE 44
### THE FLY-BY-NIGHTS

Inside the phone box, Sir Peter discovers a carrier pigeon, together with instructions to put the diamond in a bag on its leg and release it.

## PUZZLE 45
### THE CLOCKS IN THE COLLEGE BOATHOUSE

The final clock should show a time of 7.05. Professor Alexis compares the times on clocks 1, 2, 3 and 4 and works out that clock 2 shows a time of plus one hour 50 minutes (compared to clock 1), clock 3 shows minus two hours 40 minutes (compared to clock 2), and clock 4 shows plus one hour 30 minutes (compared to clock 3). Therefore the final clock should show a time of minus two hours 20 minutes (compared to clock 4). Clock 4 shows 9.25, and two hours 20 minutes before 9.25 is 7.05.

## PUZZLE 46
### HIDDEN PICTURE 2

When completed, the grid produces the image shown below. Can you come up with some truly creative ideas for what this image represents? It could be a crusader knight holding a giant key. Perhaps it's not a person at all but a floorplan for some kind of sacred building. Does it make the puzzle easier rather than harder when the shape created is not immediately recognizable? Be wary of assumptions that lead you away from seeing what is actually there.

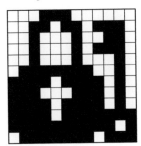

## PUZZLE 47
## LIBRARY TILES

The answer is B. Marco needs a little help from his client, who is a writer, to break the code. They work out that each letter in the top row moves forward two places in the alphabet, while those in the middle and bottom rows move backward one place in the alphabet.

| L | R | V |
|---|---|---|
| B | V | H |
| J | A | E |

## PUZZLE 48
## SYMBOL SUDOKU 3

The completed grid is shown below. Did you find the ease and speed with which you completed these symbol sudokus has improved with practise – despite the fact that they were getting progressively harder? Both these puzzles and conventional sudokus are excellent ways to build neuronal connections and boost your thinking.

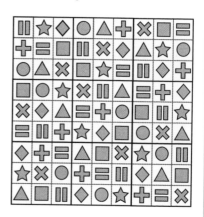

**ANSWERS**

## PUZZLE 49
## BATTLESHIPS 3

The completed battleships grid is shown below. Finding the single correct solution to this provokes an "Aha!" of pleasure – a small delight in achievement. From very early in our history, we human beings have needed to solve practical and mental problems in order to survive and progress, and a desire to solve puzzles and overcome challenges is, as a result, hardwired in our brains.

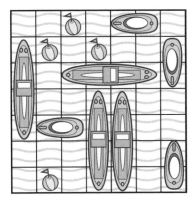

## PUZZLE 50
## PROFESSOR GREENACRE'S
## CUPCAKES

Henri divides the ellipse tray as shown. You are making good progress if you can solve these puzzles within the time limit of 5–6 minutes. If you get stuck with this type of test, try looking away or doing something else for a few minutes, then coming back to it with fresh eyes. Of course, you can "stop the clock" while you are not actually attempting the puzzle!

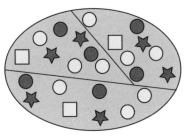

# THE CHALLENGE
# A WORKING BIRTHDAY

Your first task is to get out of the car. This is not too difficult: after a few moments it occurs to you to try the driver's door, because your driver departed in a hurry and perhaps did not lock the door when she left. It is unlocked.

Now you are outside the car. You have the letter and the cloakroom ticket. What should you do? You remember that your driver said, "See you up there!" This was a strange thing to say, and must be meaningful, you think. You look at the elevator and decide that going up is a sensible strategy.

You approach the elevator and look at the keypad beside the doors. It has numbers and letters in it. Perhaps you try punching random numbers into the pad, even your name. The doors will not open. Still the LCD display will be asking you "How did you get here? Why are you here?" One answer could be that you got there by limousine. You inspect the vehicle. Its license plate is 5 DEE 467.

You are very pleased with yourself and try keying 5 DEE 467 into the keypad. Nothing doing. But you stay calm. You reconsider the questions and consider why you are here. Is the answer that you are here to see SHOOM!? The same word is written on the limo. So you try keying the letters SHOOM. The elevator doors open!

In the elevator there is one UP button and one DOWN. You choose UP. It is a long climb, and on the way up you have time to consider the question of redeveloping the parking facility. One answer, suggested by the young men you saw skateboarding and dancing on the streets outside and by all the ramps in the parking facility, could be to redevelop the parking facility as a skateboarding centre with dance areas and food outlets.

# ANSWERS

When the elevator doors open you find yourself in the waiting area of a very plush restaurant called "Moon River". Opposite is a cloakroom area. You approach and hand in your tab.

Amazingly, the young clerk in the cloakroom hands you your briefcase. Just at that moment your driver approaches, now dressed in an expensive business suit. And before you can say anything, she introduces herself as the Managing Director of SHOOM! She asks you what your redevelopment plan is for the parking facility and seems impressed by your answer, but she asks again, "Are you sure you know why you're here?"

Then she ushers you to a table, where your three sisters are waiting. They shout "Happy Birthday!" and reveal that they planned the whole scheme as a "Birthday Adventure". But the connection to SHOOM! is genuine, they say: the Managing Director is an old friend of theirs, who named the company after their initials. They kiss you and pour you a glass of the finest champagne.

Then the Managing Director congratulates you on your calm and creative thinking in a crisis, praises your redevelopment suggestion and offers you a consultancy contract with her firm. You toast the deal and your birthday with the champagne. What a day!

# SUGGESTED READING AND RESOURCES

*A Certain Ambiguity: A Mathematical Novel* by Gaurav Suri & Hartosh Singh Bal, Princeton University Press 2007

*A Technique for Producing Ideas* by James Webb Young, McGraw-Hill Professional 2003

*A Whack on the Side of the Head: How You Can Be More Creative* by Roger Von Oech, Grand Central Publishing 2008

*Cracking Creativity: The Secrets of Creative Genius for Business and Beyond* by Michael Michalko, Ten Speed Press 2001

*Einstein's Dreams* by Alan Lightman, Time Warner 1994

*Make the Most of Your Mind* by Tony Buzan, Colt Books 1977

*Six Thinking Hats* by Edward de Bono, Penguin Books 2000

*Sticky Wisdom* by Dave Allan, Matt Kingdon, Kris Murrin and Daz Rudkin, Capstone 2002

*Take Your Time* by Eknath Easwaran, Nilgiri Press 2006

*Teach Yourself: Training Your Brain* by Terry Horne and Simon Wootton, Hodder Headline 2007

*The Creative Habit* by Twyla Tharp, Simon & Schuster 2008

*The Einstein Factor* by Win Wenger, Crown Publications 2002

"The Tremendous Adventures of Major Brown" in *The Club of Queer Trades* by G.K. Chesterton, Dover 1988. The story (and the entire book) is also available to read or download free on various websites.

*Thinkertoys: A Handbook of Creative-Thinking Techniques* by Michael Michalko, Ten Speed Press 2006

Film: *Pay It Forward* (2001), directed by Mimi Leder, based on the novel of the same name by Catherine Ryan Hyde (Black Swan 2007)

www.creativethinking.net
www.creativethinkingwith.com
www.edwdebono.com
www.imagineitproject.com
www.michaelgelb.com
www.payitforwardfoundation.org
www.winwenger.com

# THE AUTHOR

Charles Phillips is the author of 20 books and a contributor to more than 25 others, including *The Reader's Digest Compendium of Puzzles & Brain Teasers* (2001). Charles has investigated Indian theories of intelligence and consciousness in *Ancient Civilizations* (2005), probed the brain's dreaming mechanism in *My Dream Journal* (2003), and examined how we perceive and respond to colour in his *Colour for Life* (2004). He is also a keen collector of games and puzzles.